In Patrice's Purse!

By

Patrice Y. Goslee

Forward:

My heart's desire is to encourage and bring JOY, which carries us to: *In Patrice's Purse* and how this was birthed. As God continued to download various nuggets of inspiration to hold-on to and pack in my purse (heart), I was reminded of Deuteronomy 11:18 "There you shall lay these words of men in your heart and in your soul." Your purses, fanny-packs or whatever you carry, holds value. Especially what's inside! It started with posting on social media, but I chose to go bigger! I stepped out on faith and ta-daa… here I am today sharing with YOU! My mindset is – "If I can change the way I think, I can change the atmosphere where I enter!"

One last thing: Just to give you something to start your journey of speaking life: Matthew 12:34(b) NIV – "For the mouth speaks what the heart is full of." Sister to sister…I am my sister's keeper!

Glow Get Her: A driven woman who strives to reach her goals not matter what, glowing inside and out!

#KeepShining

You continue to shine! Let them talk, let them hate, let them try to figure you out. Keep shining sis!

#NeverADullDiamond

Take yourself out on a date sometimes... With your fine self!

#YouAreWorthIt

Walk with confidence. You are your own runway!

#PrettyPosture

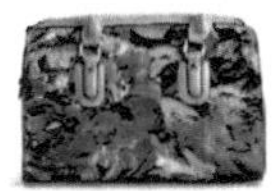

Make your day FULL of possibilities!

#BeLimitless

Rest well Sis! Know that nothing you're going through is too big for God!

#ComfortableInHim

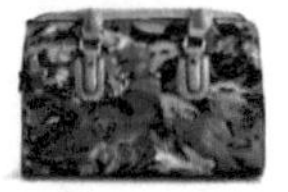

I hate absolutely nothing about me!

#SelfLoveIsTheBestLove

How bad do you want it? Fight for it in the Spirit.

#WarInWorship

Be-YOU-tiful. Don't ruin YOU by being someoyne else.

#YOUnique

Guuuurl, Celebrate! Look how far you've come!

#VictoryLap

You may not see the way, but trust that God already made the way! His process is always valid.

#FaithItOut

Look, be over apologizing for your shine! It's called FAVOR. Signed, The New Me

#FavorFollowsMe

A sistah's been there, done that, shared that, and will help you through that

#ForeverMySistersKeeper

Grown Up... I refusey to act like I use to.

#MyNextLevel

Playing miniature games no long suits me. I've graduated to another level!

#StepUp

The wait is always greater on the other side!

#WorthTheWait

Sis... I'm rooting for YOU! When you win, I win!

#WinnersCircle

Scoot, scoot. I made room for you, too!

#SisterToSister

If someone is trying to bring you down... they're already beneath you!

#StandUpAndStayThere

Belle'ame = a beautiful soul

#SoulFood

Blend in for what?!

#StayOriginal

W.W.W. – Win your War through Worship

#BattlesWounds

It's not what they said, it's what you believe!

#GodsMasterpiece

Make'em wish they treated you better!

#PrepareTheTable

Be wise: the enemy wants to keep updates on you too!

#StayAlert

God said, "He'll keep you in perfect peace", but... is your mind on Him?

#FollowThrough

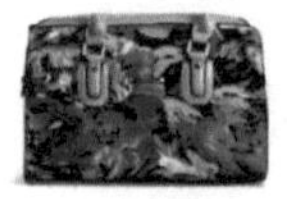

Even if it appears that everything is going sideways... keep pushing because straight forward it where God is!

#ItsFallingInPlace

Share your GLOW... You're already LIT!

#TheGlowUp

Make "detoxing" apart of your self-cleansing
from:
some people
bad habits
negative conversation
doubt
self-sabotage

You got that...vision, ambition, pursuit kinda
vibe!

#LeveledUp

Keep chin up Queen. You have a crown to keep on!

#InGoodStanding

The YOU you're becoming is waiting to be chosen.

#ChooseHer

The past is too heavy to carry in your future.
Drop "that" weight.

#BeFree

Resolved: A released battle God handled.

#PeaceOfMind

If people start to change, don't let it change "me" in you.

#NotWavered

Unlearned in learning.

#BetterBehavior

It's impossible to sink when you're grounded in God.

#SolidSoil

Some people are upset because what they said about you, privately, did not stop God from blessing you publicly.

#DestinedForGreatness

Prepare for the ninth month of birthing. What is your delivery going to be?

#FeedTheSeed

Unhealed trauma. What have you throwing away healthy connections with people who were really in your corner.

#HealFirst

I'm snatching joy all day!

#GiveMeMyStuff

Counterfeits always wear and tear, but you can always tell an authentic version because it lasts a lifetime.

#TheRealWillAlwaysReveal

Bad feet can't stand on Holy ground.

#CheckPostureOfHeart

Stay alert! Sometimes it's your friends who keeps your enemies updated about you.

#KeenTheScene

You don't need to tell your side of the story... Let time tell it!

#EyesAndEarsOpen

Empower yourself. Forgive.

#ThereIsFreedomAfterIt

Integrity is an honorable title.

#NoteToSelf

Notice the action... no just the words.

#KnowTheFruitTheyBare

Reminder... and it's working for your good!

#CarryOn

No thing or no one can resuscitate what is already covered under the blood of Jesus.

#OldNews

Who you value, you cover.

#CoverGirl

Be the woman that fixes another woman's crown without telling everyone it's crooked.

#CanYouKeepMySecret

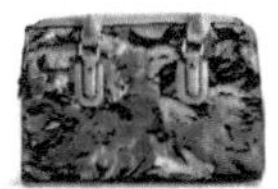

CTRL + ALT + DEL = Control your space +
Alter your prospective + Delete negative
people

#TheTrio

You up again? Get your rest...God's already
mapped out the plan!

#PieceOfPeace

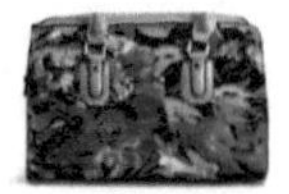

Surround yourself with those that add and multiply... place borders who subtract and divide.

#YouDoTheMath

I salute you! You showed your enemies what they tried to break, didn't work.

#StrongRoots

Stay "up". Pray up, slay up, build up, head up, speak up, step up. Live "up" to the plan God created in you.

#MovingOnUp

A leaders lingo is different. Everyone can't understand what's being said because you've elevated your vocabulary.

#WhenIMoveYouMove

Give yourself a gift. You don't even respond the way you used to!

#GrowthSpurt

...For giving me another chance to get it right.

#Grateful

A mind separated from prayer is a mind open to idols

#BondedTogether

Learn to be a good listener. Your ears will never get you in trouble.

#HearingAndHearing

Be an encourager. The world has too many
critics already.

#ADifferentApproach

And when you become a diamond, you'll see why
life pressured you.

#ApplyPressure

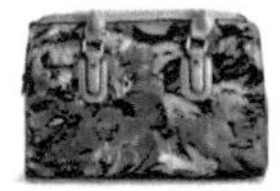

I've never seen elegance go out of style.

#ForeverTrending

The devil saw me with my head down and got excited...then I said, "Amen."

#MadeYouLook

www.ingramcontent.com/pod-product-compliance
Lightning Source LLC
Chambersburg PA
CBHW021154130726
47988CB00004B/1607